CW00969650

MAORI LEGENDS

Some myths and
legends of the Maori people
retold by
ALISTAIR CAMPBELL

Illustrated by Robin White

Viking Sevenseas Ltd; P.O. Box 152, Paraparaumu,
New Zealand

A Note on Pronunciation

Every syllable in Maori should be pronounced separately, and must end with a vowel. All consonants are sounded as they are in English, including 'wh', and 'ng' (as in 'singer').

The following is a guide for sounding the vowels: 'a' as in 'father'; 'e' as in 'egg'; 'i' as in 'machine'; 'o' as in 'order'; 'u' as in 'rude'.

If these guides are followed, even words that look difficult become quite easy to pronounce, for example, 'Murirangiwhenua' (Mu-ri-ra-ngi-whe-nu-a). Sound the syllables separately at first, then run them smoothly together.

Similarly with 'Maui' (Ma-u-i); 'Tane' (Ta-ne); 'Hakawau' (Ha-ka-wa-u); etc.

ISBN 085467 017 3
© Copyright 1969
VIKING SEVENSEAS LIMITED
P.O. Box 152, Paraparaumu, New Zealand
PRINTED IN HONG KONG
Thirteenth Printing 2007

Contents

Introduction

The myths and legends of the Maori are as fascinating as any in the world. If they do not have the graces of, say, the myths and legends of Greece, this is undoubtedly all to the good, because it probably means that they have not suffered to any great extent from the refining hands of professional story-tellers. The stories as we have them are probably much as they have been for many generations. The best of them, notably those about Maui, are true myths, disturbingly expressive of the deepest fears, needs and aspirations of the Maori people.

The one possible exception, it seems to me, is the story of Hinemoa, and this may account for its great popularity. Rightly or wrongly, I feel that it has suffered from having passed through the Mid-Victorian sentimental tradition. Its *Romeo and Juliet* elements must have made it immediately attractive to the missionaries and settlers who first heard it, and it would not have been surprising if they had softened down the starkness of the original. It nevertheless deserves its fame, and I only hope that in my much modified version I have retained some of its haunting qualities.

The creation myths of the Maori are singularly interesting in that they go back much further into the void of pre-existence than do the myths of any other race. In the space available all I can do is to give a very brief summary.

According to tradition, in the beginning was Te Kore or The Nothing, which corresponds to primeval chaos in western mythology. Te Kore existed in a state of timeless perfection until (it is never explained how) it gave birth to the First Nothing, and by this act set in motion the process of creation which resulted after many aeons in the emergence of Rangi and Papa, the original parents of gods and men, and the first in the long line of created beings to have features that were recognisably human.

Rangi and Papa clung together in a close embrace, and soon they had given birth to six male children. The children began to grow, and it was not long before they began to resent being confined between their parents' bodies. They longed for space and light, which they sensed they would enjoy once they were free.

And so they plotted to separate their parents and bring about the world order that is still in existence today. The plotters were the six sons: Tawhirimatea, the god of the winds; Tane, the god of the forests; Tu, the god of war; Tangaroa, the god of the sea; Rongo, the god of the *kumara* (the sweet potato); and Haumia, the god of the fern root.

Legend has it that the brothers quarrelled violently, and that Tawhirimatea was opposed to the separation, and that when it was over he decided to make his home in the sky with his father Rangi. The thunder and lightning are signs that he is still angry.

The act of separation was performed by Tane, who forced Rangi upwards with his feet, while his hands pressed against the ground. This act is plainly symbolic of the growth of a tree: the legs and feet are the branches, while the hands are the roots.

Rangi (the Sky) and Papa (the Earth) were finally separated and they have remained thus ever since. The falling rain and the rising mist are signs that they are still mourning for each other.

The gods next set about creating the creatures and plants of earth; and finally, they turned their attention to man. But they themselves were all male; therefore they had to create a female. They did this by taking clay from the body of their mother, Papa, and making a figure that resembled themselves.

It was left to Tane to breathe life into the nostrils of this first woman, and, later, to marry her daughter, Hinetitama, the Dawn Maiden, from whom the human race has descended.

How Maui obtained the Magic Jawbone

Maui was restless. As was his custom, when preoccupied, he paced up and down in front of his mother's house, frowning in concentration. On seeing him so withdrawn, his friends debated among themselves what to do to raise his spirits. But something in his face, so stern and forbidding, held them back. Even the village dogs slunk past, as if expecting him to turn on them without warning, and send them yelping with a kick.

What was the cause of his unrest? His mother, wiser than all women, had her suspicions, but she sighed and went on with her basket weaving, and said nothing.

Maui turned at the end of his walk and irritably whacked his thigh with his greenstone club. Ground to a translucent edge, superbly polished, it was a deadly weapon—fit for the greatest warrior. But to Maui, the beautiful club, thonged loosely to his wrist, might well have been a child's toy, for all the pride he took in it.

Again he turned in his walk, and continued striding. Yes, it was true he had his magic spells and incantations, but what he needed most was a magic weapon—one so potent he could quell the evil spirits and demons that thronged the bush and the fishing places, and made man's life intolerable.

While pacing up and down he had noticed a couple of women leaving the village by a little used path. They were carrying baskets of food that gave off steam in the cool morning air. He thought no more about it, until, later in the day, he saw them coming back empty-handed. Next day the same thing happened, and the day after that. Each time they left with food, and came back empty-handed.

His curiosity aroused, Maui went up and asked them: "To whom did you take the food?"

The servants looked at each other quickly, and said nothing.

"Answer me," said Maui, angrily.

"Oh, Maui," said the elder of the two, "it is not for us to tell you. We are but servants, acting under orders. If you must know, then you must ask your mother."

Maui dismissed them with an impatient wave of his club, and went to look for Taranga. He found her working with her women. At his approach, they rose like a flock of geese and hurried away, leaving the two together.

"Oh, Maui," said Taranga, "I have been expecting you. Sit down beside me."

Maui sat down beside her, and then said, "Mother, I have to know. To whom are the servants taking food?"

"Maui," said his mother, "The time has come for me to tell you. The food was for Murirangiwhenua, your blind grandmother. As long as she is fed, she is contented and does not trouble us. But if we forget to feed her, she goes mad with hunger. The servants, that you spoke to, see that she is fed. That is their sacred duty. Should they forget to feed her—even once—they would have to pay with their lives. They themselves would be thrown to the old woman who would eat them alive."

Then Maui said, "Where is she, this old woman?"

"She is over there," said his mother, pointing to the path that had been taken by the servants.

"How shall I know her?"

"You will know her by her jawbone," said his mother. "Maui, that is the weapon you are looking for. It has great magical powers. With that in your hand, my son, nothing can withstand you."

Maui's mind was made up. Nothing must stand in his way. He had to possess the jawbone.

And so, next morning, he met the servants on the little used path, just as they were setting out.

"Give me the food," he said. "Your work is done. From now on I shall take her the food."

They handed over the baskets without a word, and returned to the village. Maui went on down the path until at last he

8

came to the old woman's house. She was sitting in the porch on a pile of human bones, her blind eyes closed, her great jaw lifted, as she sniffed the air. The huge head turned towards him, but he had taken care to be down wind, and so she did not detect him.

Carefully, so that she would not hear, he placed the food some distance away from her, and then returned to the village. The next day he returned, and again he placed the food beyond her reach. By the third day she was aware that some one was playing tricks on her, and on the following day, when he arrived with her food, she was waiting for him. She sniffed the air, and began to distend her stomach to swallow him.

At first she sniffed to the south, but she could sense nothing there. She growled in disappointment, and began sniffing to the north, but again she detected nothing. She then sniffed to the east, her nostrils quivering, but again there was nothing. Thoroughly aroused, her stomach fully distended, she turned to the west and sniffed. Ah! She had detected him!

She sniffed again to make sure, then cried in a loud voice: "You over there! Are you from the direction of the wind that blows on my skin?"

Maui coughed to say that he was.

The old woman therefore knew that he could only be a relative, and her stomach began to subside. If he had not come from the west, she would have swallowed him at once.

"Are you Maui then?" she asked.

"Yes," he admitted.

"Then you must be my grandson," she said. "But if that is so, why do you practise your childish tricks on me?"

"I have come for your jawbone," was all that he said in reply, "and I must have it."

"Take it, and welcome," said the old woman. "I have been keeping it for you. But before you take it, let me give you a warning. Do not wash it clean in the river, for the fish will gather round for the morsels you scrape off. No, wash it on dry land, far away from any stream."

Then Maui went up to her, took hold of her lower jaw and wrenched it free. He remembered her words, and did not wash it clean until he felt that he could safely do so. He then shook water from his calabash on to the jawbone and scraped off the bits of flesh that clung to it, until it glowed white in the morning sun.

Rejoicing in his weapon, Maui gripped it firmly and swung it round his head several times, so that it seemed to sing in a thin high-pitched voice. And what the jawbone sang of, Maui's enemies were soon to learn.

But even as he stood there, trying out his weapon, the water he had used was hurrying down the hillside. It was to carry the blood down to the river, where the fish were to gather round and feed on it.

Thus it came about that the fish, known to the Maoris as *kokopu*, obtained its reddish colouring from the blood of Murirangiwhenua, the grandmother of Maui.

Maui nooses the Sun

Maui went home to his village with the magic jawbone, and lived with his brothers. It was everything he required of a weapon. Even to hold it gave him such a sense of power that it was easy for him to believe he was invincible. Why, sometimes he had the feeling that he could challenge the sun himself, and come out the victor!

Ah, the sun! How hateful he had become! Even now, as Maui watched, he was racing across the sky—a huge red ball of fire that scorched the leaves and dried up the lakes and streams.

The days had become so short that the people never had time to till the fields or lay in supplies of food. Each day it was the same. The men would shoulder their tools and make their way to the fields. But they had scarcely begun the day's work, before the sun had passed his zenith and was taking his downward path. Then, while they watched helplessly, he would rapidly sink in the west, plunging the world into darkness.

They had once prayed to the gods for help, but help had never come. Then they had sunk into misery and despair, and kept their eyes on the ground, and never uttered a word.

Maui noticed these things and was deeply troubled. It was then that he thought of a way to help mankind, but he could not act alone. He must persuade his brothers to help him. He found them lying in the shade, only their eyes moving, as they watched the sun careering across the sky.

"My brothers, listen to me. The sun must be slowed down. If he continues at such a reckless pace the villagers will all die."

But Maui's brothers laughed. "Little brother, what are you planning to do?"

"I plan to teach him a lesson," said Maui, "so that never again will he cause suffering by going so fast.

Then his brothers scoffed at him. "Take care, little brother, the sun will eat you up, and afterwards spit the bones out."

"You laugh at me now," said Maui, "but later on you will thank me."

Despite themselves, his brothers were impressed. Their faces grew serious, and they gathered round him, all talking at once.

"But no one can go near the sun."

"Its heat is too great."

"You'll be cooked to a cinder."

"Maui, give up your scheme. It's madness."

It was now Maui's turn to laugh. "I have never failed in my life, so why should I fail now? Have I ever been outwitted? Can I not change myself into a bird, and back again into a man, while you, my brothers, must always remain in your present form?"

"It is true, Maui," said his brothers, "that you have done great deeds, but you have always counted on your tricks and magic spells for your success. What if they prove to be powerless against the sun?"

"Enough," said Maui. "We are wasting time." He raised his magic jawbone, and his brothers gazed at it in wonder. "It is the jawbone of our grandmother, and when I beat the sun with it he will yell for mercy."

"What can we do to help?" asked the brothers.

"Well, first there are ropes to be plaited," said Maui. "They have to hold back the sun, so they must be stronger than any ropes have ever been."

Then the brothers set to work, determined to produce the ropes that were needed. They used all their skill and cunning, and, in so doing, they discovered how to plait the strong square-shaped rope, the flat rope and the round rope. At the end of the day, coils of rope lay ready for the adventure ahead.

Next morning, Maui and his brothers set off towards the east. They were weighed down by the ropes, so they made slow progress. But they came at last one evening to the edge of the pit from which the sun was to rise. Nothing lived in that place. Everything had been blasted because of its closeness to the sun.

"This is the place," said Maui. "Come, my brothers. Before the sun appears, we have much work to do."

The brothers set to work, and all around the pit they put in posts. They then strung ropes across to form a giant web, and at the centre Maui placed a noose made from the strongest rope.

They had just finished their net, when the first rays of the sun appeared at the bottom of the pit.

"Now remember," said Maui urgently, "do nothing to startle the sun. If you do, we have lost him. Just let him ease his head into the noose, then haul on the ropes as hard as you can." His brothers nodded assent, and then they waited.

The rays grew brighter and brighter as the sun rose up the pit. Now his head appeared and gave off such a glare that the brothers covered their eyes. Slowly he rose until his shoulders were held by the net and his head was in the noose. He knew at once he was trapped and began to struggle desperately.

"Pull hard," shouted Maui, then seizing the magic jawbone he leapt on to the sun and began to beat him.

"Maui, let me go," bellowed the sun, but Maui went on beating him.

"I am a terrible fellow, Maui, I warn you. You'll be sorry if you don't let me go." But still Maui went on beating him.

"Maui," cried the sun, growing weaker, "say what you want me to do, and I shall do it—but please stop beating me."

"Very well," said Maui, "but let that be a lesson to you. By your mad haste across the sky you have made the days too short, and caused much suffering. If you promise not to go so fast, we shall untie the ropes and let you go."

The sun made a solemn promise and was allowed to go.

As he limped painfully up the sky, he called back, "Oh Maui, I ache all over. What was the weapon that you beat me with?"

"The jawbone of my grandmother," said Maui.

"I might have known it," groaned the sun. "It has robbed me of half my power."

"It is well for you that it did," said Maui. "Now men will look on you, not as an enemy but as a friend."

And so it turned out. The sun went slowly across the sky, and its rays were mild and beneficent. The villagers now had time to till their fields and to do their chores. The earth became fruitful, and singing and laughter was heard again throughout the land.

The Great Fish of Maui

One morning, while it was still dark, Maui's brothers rose silently from their sleeping mats and hurried down to the beach, thinking that Maui was asleep. But their furtive movements and whispered talk had woken him, and he stole after them, and stood back in the shadows and listened to them talking, as they prepared their canoe for a fishing trip.

"It is well that we left Maui asleep," said one.

"It is indeed," said another. "But he can be a most useful fellow to have around. I have seen him grab a whale by its tail and drag it high on the beach."

"That may be so," said a third, "but we dare not have him with us when we go fishing, for he is a mischief-maker and may play tricks on us."

The brothers then pushed their canoe into the water and paddled out to sea, leaving Maui determined that next time, come what may, he would go fishing with them.

In the evening his brothers returned empty-handed and, thinking that they were unobserved, they dragged their canoe up the beach and hid it in thick bush. But Maui marked the place and, before dawn, he concealed himself under the seats where his brothers would not see him.

Soon afterwards they arrived, and, after the usual preparations, they put out to sea. They had paddled a long way from the land when Maui decided that it was time to reveal himself. He rose from his hiding place and greeted his brothers, who were too astonished to speak.

"It is a fine day for fishing, is it not? If you will bear with me, my brothers," he said, "perhaps your luck may change."

The brothers were angry to find him aboard. "We are not far from land," said one, "let us turn round, and return him to shore."

They started to turn their canoe round, but while they were doing this, Maui muttered a powerful incantation, at once causing the land to become so distant that only the mountain ranges could be seen.

The brothers looked at each other in surprise. "We have come further than we realised," they said. "It is too far to go back now. What is to be done with him?"

"Why not take me with you?" said Maui. "You may need me to bail out the canoe."

They agreed reluctantly, and began to paddle further out to sea, until they reached an ancient fishing place. There they stopped, and ordered Maui to throw the anchor out.

"No," said Maui. "This is not the place. We must go further out."

The brothers grumbled, but they went on paddling, until at last they reached another fishing place, more ancient than the first.

"This is the place," they said to Maui. "Now throw the anchor out."

"No," said Maui. "This is not the place. Where the water is too shallow, the fish are not worth catching. We must go further still, and let our anchor down in the deepest part of the sea."

Once more they paddled on, until their arms and shoulders ached, and it seemed they could go no further. But Maui kept urging them on.

"We are almost there, my brothers. The mountains are barely visible now. The moment they disappear, we shall know that we have arrived."

Thus Maui and his brothers reached at last the most ancient of fishing places, and there the anchor was dropped. Then the brothers let down their lines, and before they had touched the bottom there was a fish on every hook. Again they let down their lines, and, after they pulled them up, the canoe was full of fish.

Excited by their wonderful catch, the brothers said to Maui, "Let us return to land."

16

But Maui said, "Not yet, I have some fishing to do."

His brothers laughed and said, "What can a fellow like you catch? Why, you haven't even a hook!"

"What is this then?" he replied, and laughed at the astonished looks on their faces, when they saw the hook that he had taken from under his cloak.

It was decorated with *paua* shell and a tuft of dog's hair, and as he turned it in his hand it flashed in the sunlight. It was so fine a hook that each brother longed to own it. What they did not know was that a chip of their grandmother's jawbone, attached to the barb, gave it magical powers.

"True, that is a hook," they said. "But what use is it without bait?"

"I had hoped," said Maui quietly, "that you would give me some."

"What! Give *you* bait?" said the brothers. "*That* we shall never do."

"So be it," said Maui. He clenched his fist and struck himself on the nose and as the blood ran down, he smeared his fish-hook with it, and then let it down into the water, where it became hooked in the doorway of a meeting-house.

Then Maui braced his feet and began to pull on the line. Sweat poured from his body, as he slowly hauled up the great fish. The gable broke the surface, then the sea for miles around was disturbed, as the enormous body of the fish came into view.

Then Maui's brothers threw up their hands and began to wail. "Oh, Maui, you are to blame for our misfortunes. You brought us here, far from the land, against our wishes. Now a god rises from the depths of the sea, angry at being disturbed. He will devour us, and not even our bones will survive his anger."

But Maui did not hear them. He was chanting an incantation which caused the fish to become placid and the waves to subside. Then he continued hauling on the line, until the fish lay still on the surface, with the canoe raised high and dry on its back. Maui had fished up the North Island of New Zealand, traditionally known for this reason as *Te Ika a Maui* (The Fish of Maui). If you look at a map you will see that its shape resembles that of a fish.

Maui stepped out of the canoe and looked about him. He saw a small village nearby, a group of people standing round a fire, and children playing.

He turned to his brothers and said proudly, "This is a fine fish I have caught. Now I must go and make an offering to the gods. When I come back, we shall cut up the fish and share it equally among us. But meanwhile, my brothers, do nothing to injure the fish."

The brothers promised to obey him, but no sooner had he left them than they began to cut up the fish and eat it. The fish writhed and twisted, but the brothers never let up. They sliced, they hacked, they chopped, until the entire surface of the fish had become jagged and mutilated.

Thus, through the greed and disobedience of the brothers, were formed the cliffs, valleys, plains and mountain ranges of the North Island. If they had listened to their brother's words, the island would have been smooth and level to this day—as smooth and level as Maui's fish had been.

Maui and the Fire Goddess

One morning, bent on mischief, Maui stole like a shadow through the sleeping villages, putting out all the fires. Then back to his own house he went and waited for the dawn. Before long, people began to stretch and yawn. They came out of their stuffy, low-built houses, into the sunlight, rubbing their eyes, as they busied themselves with their morning chores.

Then Maui rose, pretending that he had just awoken, and began shouting at his servants. "Ho, there! Be quick and bring me food. I am faint with hunger." He smiled slyly to himself as his servants rushed off to carry out his orders.

They went to their usual fireplace, but what they saw there puzzled them. Instead of flickering flames, they saw cold ashes and blackened embers. From all parts of the village the servants came rushing, each with the same story to tell, all the fires were out. What was to be done? How was food to be cooked? How were the villagers to keep warm? Excited groups began to form, as uneasiness began to spread.

Now messengers began to arrive. From villages far and near came the same story. Uneasiness turned to alarm, and alarm to panic, when it became plain that every fire in the land was out.

Then Maui's mother, Taranga, came out of her house and spoke to the villagers. "My friends, be calm. We'll soon replace the fire that we have lost. When that time comes, your hearths will blaze once more, and your ovens simmer. Meanwhile, be patient."

Then Taranga turned to her servants, and commanded them to go to the lower world, to the house of Mahuika, and fetch

fire from her. But they would not go, so greatly did they fear her.

Then Maui spoke: "This is a deed for a hero, not for servants with the shrinking hearts of children. Mother, I will go and fetch fire, but by what path shall I go?"

When she heard him speak, Taranga grew afraid for him, but she answered firmly. "Go by the main path, my son, and, sooner than you think it possible, you will come to her. If she questions you, mention your name, and she will know you— for are you not her grandson? But I warn you: do not practise any tricks on her. It would be very dangerous, and I might lose a son. You are a tricky fellow, Maui. There is no one trickier in the world. That's why I warn you."

Maui followed her directions and took the main path to the lower world. By evening he had left the light of day far behind him, and had entered the cave that led to Mahuika, the fire goddess. Already he felt her presence, and, though he was brave and cunning, he began to tremble, for her breath was like a forest fire that surges through the tree tops, leaving behind it blackened stumps and smoking ashes.

Maui plucked up his courage and cried out: "Old woman, rise. Where is the fire that I have come to get?"

Mahuika rose, and, though she was old beyond belief, Maui was struck dumb with wonder, for her eyes showered with sparks and her skin shimmered like embers breathed on by the wind.

"Who is this man?" she asked.

"It is I," said Maui.

"I do not know you," she replied. "Where are you from?"

"From this country."

"Your looks tell me you lie," she said. "I say you're from the north."

"No," he said emphatically.

"Then you are from the east."

"No."

"Are you from the west then?"

"No."

"Then are you from the direction of the wind that blows upon my skin?"

"Yes," said Maui.

"Ah," said the goddess, stretching out her hand, "then you are my grandson Maui. Welcome. But what do you want from me?"

"I have come to get fire from you."

"You are welcome to it," said Mahuika. "Here it is."

Maui watched in wonder as she plucked the burning nail from her little finger and gave it to him. He thanked her and went away. But he had not gone far, when he killed the flame by plunging it in water. Then he returned to Mahuika and said, "Old woman, the fire that you gave me has gone out."

"How did it go out?" asked the goddess.

"I fell into a stream," said Maui. "Give me another nail, and I shall leave you in peace."

The unsuspecting goddess grumbled a little, but plucked a nail from another finger and gave it to him. Maui went away, and this one also he plunged into the stream.

Then he went back for another. He repeated this performance until the goddess had plucked out all her fingernails, and had started on her toes. Before long all the toes, except one, had also been stripped of their nails.

But by now the goddess was aware that Maui was up to his tricks, and when he came to ask her for her very last nail, she turned on him in a rage.

"Oh no, you trickster, Maui! I have found you out. Now you will pay with your life for your trickery!"

With that, she seized her remaining nail and flung it at his feet, where it burst into fire. Maui turned and fled, but the flames roared after him.

Nowhere was he safe from the fury of Mahuika. He turned into a fish and sought refuge in the sea, but almost at once the water began to boil. Then he changed into a hawk and soared high into the air, but the terrible flames reached after him and scorched his feathers.

At last in his terror he called on the gods for help, and these were the words of his prayer:

> "Give water to me
>   To put the fire out
>   Which is pursuing me!"

Then Tawhirimatea, the god of the winds, took pity on him and sent his children to help him. The lightning flashed and the thunder rolled, and from every region of the sky the clouds came rumbling to Maui's aid. Then the rain came down in floods upon the fire—the long rain, the heavy rain, the lasting rain. The flames hissed and roared, but were battered down at last by the rain.

Now it was Mahuika's turn to flee, and terror lent speed to her feet. But swift as she was, the angry floods were swifter. They chased her through the world, caught her up and drowned her.

So relentless was the rain, it threatened to put out every particle of fire on the earth. It was Maui who recognised this danger, and by his actions guaranteed that man would never be without fire.

He took a flame and hid it in the *kaikomako* tree, where the water could not reach it. There it has slept ever since in perfect safety, waking into new life whenever man required its services.

In the old days, when the Maori wanted fire, they would take two dry pieces of this wood and rub one on the other, until the friction they produced set free the flame that once lived in the big toe of Mahuika.

Maui and the Death Goddess

"What is the trouble, Maui?" asked Makea one evening. It was unusual to see his son so moody. He shook his head in wonder, and smiled.

"Father," said Maui, "even as we sit here talking, the children of men are treading the gloomy path to death."

"All men are doomed to die," said Makea. "Sooner or later they drop as ripe fruit from the tree, and are gathered up by Hinenuitepo—the Great Mother of Night."

Maui stood up impatiently, and began pacing up and down, "But must it always be so? If Death were to die, would man not live forever?"

Makea looked troubled. "Listen to me, my son, and take warning. Such thoughts are dangerous. No man can conquer Death."

"You talk of an ordinary man, Father. If that man were I —what then?"

Makea sighed deeply. "Maui, like any ordinary man you too must die."

"How can that be?" said Maui. "Did not my mother prophesy that I would live forever? No ordinary man can do what I have already done. Did I not conquer fire, subdue the sun—yes, and even fish up land from the sea?"

He slapped his chest boastfully. "What is Death to me but another adversary to outwit."

Then Makea spoke sharp words to him. "You are not in the upper world now, but in the lower world where your cunning may not help you." He frowned and then went on. "It is true, my son, that your mother prophesied that you would live for-

ever, but what I now have to say will come as a shock to you." He looked sadly at his son, who had stopped pacing and was watching him intently. "When I baptised you, my mind went blank as a child's and I left out a passage of the incantation. By this omission, Maui, I undid the prophesy. That is how I know that you must die."

For once Maui was speechless. He stood with folded arms and stared for a long time at his father. At last he said, "Will this be by Hinenuitepo?"

"Yes, my son."

Maui nodded thoughtfully. "So be it. The fates give me no choice, but to try to conquer Death, even if I should die." With these words, Maui became again his usual confident self. "Father, what is she like—this Hinenuitepo?"

"She is terrible beyond imagination," said his father. "Those are her eyes that you see flashing on the horizon. They are as dark as greenstone. Her teeth are sharp as obsidian, and she has the malevolent grin of a barracuda. Her hair floats round her face like kelp. In all things she is monstrous, except her body, which is like that of an old woman."

Then a plan took seed in Maui's mind, and a gleam came into his eyes. Makea saw that gleam and was troubled, because he knew that once again Maui was plotting one of his tricks. But he kept his fears to himself, knowing that no advice had any effect on Maui once he had made up his mind.

Already he mourned for Maui in his heart: "Farewell, my last born and power of my old age, for truly you were born to die."

But, even before his father was out of sight, Maui's plans were complete. Its very outrageousness seemed to assure him of success. Pleased with his cunning, Maui laughed aloud. He would have been less pleased with himself had he known that his laughter had reached as far away as Hinenuitepo and had wakened her. Lightning flashed about her head, as she rolled her eyes sleepily. Her voice boomed ominously like the sea in a cave.

"Can that be Maui?" she grumbled. "How can he laugh when he must know that even now I wait for him? It is pre-ordained that he must die—but he is a tricky fellow, and the fate of Mahuika warns me not to take him lightly." And so, still grumbling, she went back to sleep.

Meanwhile, Maui was busy putting his scheme into action. As success depended on the co-operation of the forest creatures, he decided to take them into his confidence. The teeming folk of Tane that lived in the trees and on the forest floors flocked to hear his words. Tits, robins, saddlebacks, grey warblers, fantails, silver eyes, even the tiny rifleman, the smallest bird of the forest, all were told of his plans and the part that they must play.

Then, certain of success, Maui set off with his companions. As they drew ever closer to the sleeping goddess, the gay chatter of the birds gradually died away, until not a sound was heard except the subdued flutter of many wings and the rustle of feet on the fallen leaves. There was now a chill in the air. It grew more intense as Maui passed through the bent and sickly trees, bearded with lichen, that bordered on the clearing where the goddess lay. Maui shivered and drew his feathered cloak closer about him. There she lay in the doorway of her house just as his father had described her. The terrible eyes were lidded, but the lower jaw slack with sleep, hung down, exposing the obsidian teeth in a permanent grin. As she breathed out heavily, an icy draught swept across the clearing.

Maui held up his hand as a signal for the birds to stop, then in an urgent whisper he spoke to them. "My little friends, there she lies asleep—Hinenuitepo, the Great Mother of Night. I ask you to remember my words, for my life is in your hands. I will enter her body, but on no account must you laugh until I have passed through her body and come out through her mouth. Then you can laugh, if you must. But if you laugh before then, I shall die."

Then the birds were greatly agitated and they begged him to give up his plan, which now seemed crazy in the frightening presence of the goddess.

"Maui, come back to us," they cried. "Do not persist with your plan."

But Maui scoffed at their fear, and again he reminded them not to laugh too soon. Then a great sigh went up from the assembled birds, and solemnly they said, "Go then. The decision must be yours."

Then Maui approached the goddess. Quickly he took off his garments, until he stood naked, his skin shimmering in the light escaping from beneath her eyelids. Then, with a mocking smile, he stooped and quickly made his way, head first, into her body. His shoulders and then his chest soon disappeared.

The birds gasped at Maui's nimbleness. Some could not watch, but hid their heads beneath their wings. Others blinked their eyes, choking back the laughter that threatened to overwhelm them. The sound of tittering was beginning to rise like the rustle of wind through leaves, when the goddess groaned and shifted, light flashing from her eyes, as her eyelids fluttered. The twittering died away, ad the birds shrank back into the shadows, and held their breath.

But as the goddess settled down again, back they came to observe the antics of Maui, who was now thrusting his head into the throat of the goddess. Once more the birds shook with silent laughter, but thinking that victory was in sight for Maui, they desperately controlled themselves. Then Maui gave a heave, and pushed upwards with his shoulders so that his face suddenly appeared in the mouth of the goddess.

It was too much for the fantails. They burst into shrill laughter. At once the goddess woke, knew at once what was happening, and squeezed Maui to death. She closed her thighs on him, and broke his body in two.

So ended, in laughter and disgrace, Maui's attempt to conquer death, and, because of his failure, the children of men continue to tread the dark path to Hinenuitepo.

Tinirau and his Pet Whale

Tinirau was a great chief, famous throughout the land for his handsome looks and his noble bearing. But he was even better known for his school of whales.

When he called them, they would come and play off shore, cruising round in circles and blowing spray through their vent holes. His favourite was Tutunui, the largest of his whales. Tinirau liked nothing better than to climb upon his back and ride him through the breakers, and out into the stormy sea. He would look down on the flying waves and feel safe, as if he were on an island.

Now Tinirau had a son and, when the boy came of age, he wished to have him properly baptised, so that he would grow into a great warrior, like himself.

His people made special preparations for a feast, and friends from miles around arrived to take part in the celebrations. Kae, who was a priest of the highest rank, was invited to conduct the service, and on the day of the feast he and his followers arrived in a canoe.

After the service was over, there was much feasting and merriment, but at last the supplies of food ran out. Kae was about to depart when Tinirau rose and said, "Wait, there is more to eat."

Then Tinirau stood on the shore and began calling, "Tutunui, Tutunui! Come at once. I need you."

"Who are you calling?" said Kae, shading his eyes and looking out to sea. "There is nobody out there."

But Tinirau went on calling, until the sea heaved and swirled, as the huge bulk of Tutunui, streaming with water, rose into

view. Tinirau went up to him and, to Kae's astonishment, cut off a large slice of his flesh.

"He is so big," said Tinirau, "he will never miss it." He gave the flesh to the women, and they cooked it, and gave a piece to Kae, who swore that he had never eaten flesh that had tasted better.

But now it was time to go. Kae, who had an evil plan in his mind, went up to Tinirau and said, "My home is far away, and my friends must miss me. Lend me your whale so that I can get home quickly."

When Tinirau looked doubtful, Kae said, "Who baptised your son? Was it not I? Lend me your whale. It is but a small favour that I ask of you."

Tinirau was very reluctant to lend his whale, but he did not wish to offend Kae by refusing, for as well as being a priest, Kae was a magician who had the power to harm him, if he chose to.

"Very well," he said, "but you must be careful, especially as you approach land. The whale knows when it is not safe for him to go further. As soon as he gives a shake, you must get off. If you stay on his back, he will keep going until he becomes stranded in shallow water, where he will die."

"I understand," said Kae. "I shall do nothing to endanger him."

Then he climbed on to the back of the huge beast, and it seemed no time before he was approaching the shore of his village. There was his carved meeting-house looking handsome in the sunlight. There were his children running down to the shore, shouting and pointing their fingers at the strange sight of their father on the back of a whale.

He felt the whale give a shake, but he took no notice. The children were close now, and were coming closer. The whale gave another shake, but now it was too late. He had gone too far and was well and truly stranded.

What a feast was held that night in Kae's village! The rich smell of cooked flesh rose from the ovens, and was carried by the wind far along the coast to where Tinirau was standing, waiting for his pet to return.

"Alas!" he said. "That is the sweet smell of Tutunui that the north wind brings to me." And he went to his house and wept, and his sisters gathered round and wept with him.

When he had recovered from his grief, Tinirau resolved to avenge the treacherous killing of Tutunui. He ordered his sisters to go in search of Kae.

"Search every village, if you must," he said. "But find him, and bring him to me alive. Travel as entertainers, and no one will suspect the true purpose of your mission."

"We shall gladly go," said his sisters. "But you must tell us how to recognise him, for in his country there are many people."

"Kae has such crooked teeth that he is ashamed of them, and rarely opens his mouth. Therefore, to recognise him you must make him laugh."

Tinirau's sisters left by canoe. They travelled through Kae's country, performing at each village that they came to, but nowhere was there any sign of Kae.

It seemed that their search would be fruitless, and then one evening they came to a village in a remote part of the coast. As they passed through the gate, they heard the rattle of bones. Something told them that they were the bones of Tutunui rattling in recognition of their presence.

The sisters were made welcome by the people of the village, and asked to perform for them. They went into the meeting-house and there they saw a man whom they suspected was Kae himself. He was sitting at the foot of the main post that supported the ridge-pole. He was covered to the chin with mats, and his head was lowered.

Determined to make him laugh, the sisters performed their comic dances and told bawdy jokes. The audience roared with laughter but Kae's head remained lowered. They then put on their most grotesque performance, full of comic eye-rollings, grimaces, indecent gestures and contortions of the body, until even Kae could not contain himself, but burst out laughing.

The search was over! Kae's crooked teeth had given him away.

The sisters at once ceased their dance, and began to utter a powerful incantation. It grew louder and louder, until it sounded like a rushing wind, and when it died away everyone had fallen asleep—everyone, that is, except Kae. His eyes were still glinting in the flickering light from the dying fire.

But the sisters were not deceived. They went forward and shook Kae gently by the shoulder, and his head slumped forward, and two pieces of iridescent *paua* shell fell on to the ground. He had placed them in his eyes to make them believe he was still awake.

The sisters lost no time. They tied him up in a mat and carried him down to their canoe, and paddled back to their village. They took him to Tinirau's house, and placed him at the foot of the main post that supported the ridge-pole, so that when he awoke he would think he was still in his own house. Then they woke him up.

"Kae," they said, "where are you?"

Kaw woke up and said, "Why, in my own house! Where should I be?"

"Kae, look about you, and tell us again where you are."

And Kae looked about him, and nothing that he saw outside was familiar. Then he knew he was doomed, and he hung his head and began to wail. When he looked up, Tinirau was standing before him, a club raised in his hand.

Before he brought it down, he cried, "Did Tutunui make so loud a noise when you slaughtered him?"

Then Tinirau killed Kae, and afterwards ate him. And thus was Tutunui, his pet whale, amply avenged.

Rata and his Canoe

The great chief Rata needed a canoe. It had to be large and strong, able to withstand the pounding of breakers and the buffeting of heavy seas. For the journey that Rata had planned was to a distant part of the country, where, he was told, lay the bones of his father. It would be a sacred journey, for he intended to bring back his father's bones for burial in his own village.

Rata spent much time searching for a suitable tree. It had to be a noble tree, with a straight, bare trunk that rose sixty or seventy feet in the air before spreading out into branches. He searched far and wide, and then one day he found his tree. Dwarfing its companions, it stood erect as a king, surrounded by his courtiers.

He ran his eye approvingly up the massive trunk. A breeze moved gently through the leaves, sunlight broke through, and all at once Rata saw clearly the shape that his canoe would take. It was already there, imprisoned in the wood, and he alone would set it free.

Rata went back to his village. He looked through his kit of stone adzes and chisels, and carefully chose the right tools for the job. Then, well contented, he lay down on his mat and went to sleep.

Next morning he set out early, before the sun had risen high enough to touch the tree tops, and was soon at work. He took his sharpest adze and, without any ceremony, began to attack the tree. Chips began to fly as he hacked away at the base of the tree. Then suddenly the job was done. The great tree crashed with a roar through the undergrowth.

Working quickly, Rata next attacked the top part of the tree,

so that it soon fell away with all its branches, leaving the main trunk to be shaped into a canoe. Rata paused, then seeing that the sun was low in the sky, he packed up his tools and went home.

He had no sooner left, than out they came from their hiding places—the teeming multitudes of birds and insects, who are the children of Tane. Indignant at the lack of respect shown by Rata to the god of the forests they uttered this incantation:

"The chips fly,
The roots fly.
They are nearby,
They are sticking,
They become a tree again."

Immediately, with the help of the birds, the trunk stood upright on its stump and the branches returned to their former positions. Meanwhile the insects were busy. Each had a job to do. Every chip, every fragment of leaf, no matter how small, had to be put back in place. In a moment the tree was standing as before, looking as if nothing had ever happened to it.

Next morning when Rata arrived, he looked about him in bewilderment. He had come to the right place. Of this he was certain. But where was the tree that he had cut down yesterday? He looked up and rubbed his eyes. Then he looked again. He was not mistaken. The tree was standing upright, as when he first saw it. Perhaps he had only dreamt he cut it down.

No matter. He put the puzzle from his mind, and once more set to work. He cut the tree down, trimmed the branches off, and hollowed out the trunk. He worked steadily until the proud shape of a great canoe began to emerge. Then, as night was coming on, he stopped work and went back to his village.

Again, as soon as he had left, the children of Tane came hurrying out. As before, they chanted their incantation, never resting until once more the tree was back in place.

It was a very baffled man who returned next morning. He stood awhile, undecided as to what to do, then he shrugged his shoulders and once more faced the tree. The chips began to fly, and the mystery was soon forgotten in the sheer joy of carving.

Evening came all too quickly. Rata gathered his tools together and went away. But instead of going home he hid himself in some bushes, and waited.

They came from everywhere—rustling, whirring, scurrying, flying. They gathered round his canoe and chanted:

> "Leave it, leave it, O Rata.
> You have cut it ignorantly—
> The sacred grove of Tane.
> The chips fly,
> The roots fly,
> They are near,
> They are sticking,
> They become a tree again."

Rata saw the trunk stand upright and the branches rise into place. He saw a blizzard of flying chips, as the tree rapidly returned to its former shape. The mystery was explained.

He rushed out angrily and took hold of some of the creatures, as they were leaving.

"I have caught you!" he cried. "Why are you meddling with my tree?"

"The tree belongs to Tane," they replied. "You did not ask him for permission to cut it down."

Then Rata was ashamed and hung his head, and said nothing.

The children of Tane saw that he was penitent, and felt sorry for him. "Go home," they said, "and leave the tree to us. We shall build your canoe for you."

Rata then went home and slept, and when morning came he returned to the forest. There she was, exactly as he had imagined she would be, when he first saw the tree. Sixty-foot long, superbly carved and decorated, she was a canoe fit for the sacred purpose that he had in mind.

Overjoyed at his good fortune, Rata made offerings to great Tane, god of the forest, and then began preparations to move his canoe down to the sea.

Te Kanawa and the Fairies

Te Kanawa, a chief of the Waikato, listened uneasily to his uncle's warning, although he tried to shrug it off with a laugh.

"It is easy to laugh now," said his uncle, shaking his head, "but men as brave as you once spent the night on Pukemore. They were found next morning, wandering on the lower slopes of the mountain. They had gone mad."

"Have you ever seen the fairies?" asked Te Kanawa.

"No—but I have heard they are not like us. Their hair and skin are light in colour, and their eyes are blue. They wind along the bush tracks in their thousands, their voices endlessly shrilling, like cicadas on a sun-lit hillside."

"What do you want me to do?" asked Te Kanawa. "Give up the kiwi hunt?"

"All that I ask, Te Kanawa," said his uncle, "is that you leave the mountain before dark."

Soon afterwards Te Kanawa left for Pukemore, with a party of hunters and dogs. As he made his way up the steep bush tracks, his uncle's words were so much on his mind that he kept glancing uneasily about him. Then the first kiwi was flushed out by the dogs, and the hunt was on.

In the excitement that followed, the fairies were forgotten. The hours passed quickly, with the dogs barking, and the hunters dashing after them through the undergrowth and then crying out in triumph as they captured the brown wingless birds, which they prized for their feathers.

Then, suddenly, Te Kanawa realised to his horror that it was growing dark. Too late now to go down the mountain! In half an hour it would be too dark to see the track. He thought of the sheer bluffs and deep ravines that they had passed on the way up, and decided that they had no choice but to spend the night on the mountain. As for the fairies—well it was better not to think of them!

It was now growing cold as well as dark, and so Te Kanawa and his party built a fire, cooked and ate some kiwi flesh, and then lay down between the enormous roots of a very large tree.

The others were soon asleep, but Te Kanawa lay awake for a while, watching the firelight flickering on the tree trunks. The cry of a kiwi caused his pulse to leap, and he reached for his greenstone club and took it under his mat. The familiar feel of the cold worn handle was very comforting, and, still gripping it, he fell asleep.

It was the dogs that heard them first. They began to whimper and move about restlessly, waking up all the party. Then Te Kanawa heard them, and, from the frightened looks on his companions' faces, he knew that they had also heard them. Although almost paralysed with fear, he forced himself to throw wood on the fire. The flames flared up, and he noticed that the dogs, which had stopped whimpering, were trembling uncontrollably under some bushes.

They were coming nearer!

At first Te Kanawa had heard only the high-pitched humming sound of thousands of voices that distance had merged together, but now he could distinguish many different voices—all shrill, all excited.

Laughing, shouting, screaming, they swarmed about the camp until they had surrounded it—then they fell silent. Te Kanawa found this far more frightening than the uproar.

There they were—just as his uncle had described them! Inquisitive as birds, they were pressing forward to get a good look at him. Te Kanawa jumped to his feet and threw more wood on the fire. A ripple of annoyance passed through the throng, as the flames drove them back.

But, regardless of the flames, they began to press forward once again, until they stood in a circle round Te Kanawa, looking at him with obvious pleasure. Then, chattering excitedly, they withdrew, allowing others to come forward. Before long the hordes of fairies were milling around in their eagerness to look at him.

Te Kanawa was extremely handsome, but it never occurred to him that his appearance might be the cause of their admiring glances. He thought the fairies had been attracted by the jewels he was wearing. They were priceless family heirlooms and he hated the thought of having to part with them. But he sensed a growing menace, and he was convinced that he had no time to lose if he were to prevent something terrible happening to him and his companions.

A hush came over the assembly as he undid his greenstone earrings and placed them on the ground. He placed beside them his beautiful greenstone *tiki*, the little carved figure that he wore round his neck. Then very carefully, so as not to cause alarm, he seized a stick and with it gently pushed the jewels towards the nearest group of fairies.

"Ah!" The huge assembly cried out in pleasure. Then they came forward, cautiously at first, then helter-skelter, all gesticulating, laughing and talking eagerly.

They paused as they approached the jewels, then their leaders fell on their knees, reached down and picked up, not the jewels themselves, but their *shadows*. They murmured reverently as they gazed upon them, then they passed them back to their followers. The shadows of the jewels were quickly passed from hand to hand amid a chorus of delighted exclamations, until they had disappeared into the back of the crowd.

Te Kanawa was never quite sure what happened next. In a moment he and his companions found themselves alone. The dogs got up and stretched, then lay down again, as if nothing had ever happened. Te Kanawa was suddenly very tired. He pulled his mat about him, yawned and was soon asleep.

They wasted no time getting off the mountain in the morning with their precious feathers. The kiwis multiplied, and there was always a demand for their feathers, which were used in making mats for high-born chiefs and their families, but Te Kanawa and his companions never again set foot on Pukemore.

Kahukura and the Fairy Fishermen

For some time now Kahukura had been troubled by a recurring dream. In it he heard a voice as thin as a grasshopper's, urging him to go to the far north to a place called Rangiaowhia, near the lands of the Rarawa people.

At last he could bear it no longer: he had to leave at once. He made his decision known to his family, then, disregarding their cries of warning, he set out on a journey that was to take him many days.

In time he arrived at Rangiaowhia, and was walking along the beach early one morning when he came to a place where people had been cleaning mackerel. He stopped and marvelled at the piles of entrails that littered the sand for many yards around.

"The people of this place must be marvellous fishermen," he thought to himself. "The remains indicate a very large catch of fish—much larger than any I have heard of."

He was about to walk on, when suddenly he bent down, a puzzled look on his face.

"Strange!" he thought. "These remains are quite fresh. It is too early for the fish to have been caught today, so they must have been caught last night."

A chill went up his spine, and he looked uneasily about him. There was only the long empty beach, with the wet sand at the water's edge shining in the early sun.

Kahukura knelt and examined the footmarks, and his suspicions were confirmed. They were long and narrow and lightly imprinted in the sand.

"These are the footmarks of the fairy folk," he said, standing up. He was frightened, but at the same time intensely excited, because he realised that he had stumbled on an important discovery.

And so, instead of going back to the village where he was staying, he decided to spend the night in the sandhills, from where he could keep an eye on the beach.

He was woken by thin excited voices: "Haul in the net! Haul in the net!"

Kahukura looked down and saw hundreds of slender figures bracing their feet in the sand and singing joyfully, as they hauled in the net. Although half-fainting with terror, he cautiously approached the fairies and began hauling with them. He relied on the colour of his skin, which was almost as light as that of the fairies, to save him from discovery.

"Let down the net in the sea at Rangiaowhia," they cried, "and haul it in at Mamaku."

They called out excitedly as a canoe was driven on to the sand, and a group of fairies, who had completed their task of dropping the net, rushed to help them.

All night Kahukura worked alongside the fairies, until, just before dawn, all the fish had been hauled ashore.

Immediately the fairies dropped the net and began to collect the fish. But instead of sorting them into equal piles, one for each fisherman present, as men do, they rushed about, each one grabbing the best fish for himself.

As they strung the fish together by threading lengths of flax through the gills, they kept urging each other along:

"Hurry, all of you! Time is running out. All the fish must be collected before the sun comes up."

Kahukura worked as hard as the rest, and before long he had a string full of fish. He went to lift them up, but their weight forced apart the slipknot he had cunningly tied at the end of the string, and the fish fell to the sand.

The fairies laughed good-naturedly, and one of them came up to Kahukura, pointed at the end of the string, and tied a knot in it.

He had no sooner gone away than Kahukura untied the knot, and tied another slipknot in its place. He then began stringing his fish as before, and again, when he lifted them up, they fell to the ground. The fairies once more paused and laughed, and another one of them came to his rescue.

He kept repeating this trick, thereby causing so many delays that the sun rose before the fairy fishermen had finished their work. On seeing that Kahukura was a man, they shrieked and fled in confusion, leaving their entire catch of fish, their canoes which turned out to be nothing more than pieces of dried flax stems, and, most important of all, their net of flax.

Thus Kahukura acquired the first fishing net, and from a close study of it he soon discovered how the fairy fishermen had woven it. This knowledge he passed on to his son, and soon it had spread to every part of New Zealand. The Maori people have been using fishing nets ever since.

The Magical Wooden Head

The magical wooden head! Frightening things were told of it: it could kill from a distance, suddenly and without warning; to hear even its slightest whisper meant sudden death!

The more credulous of the neighbouring villagers believed that it was a flesh-eating monster whose fury could be appeased only by the bodies of an army of its victims.

Not even Tawhirimatea, the god of the winds, who delighted in bringing terror into the hearts of his victims with his thunderbolts, commanded so much awe and respect. It even became a kind of bogeyman that mothers found useful as a deterrent to bad behaviour.

'If you don't behave yourselves," they would warn their children, "the wicked wooden head will come and eat you up!"

In spite of its fearful reputation, men coveted the wooden head for the magical powers it possessed. If they could capture it and take it home, it would set up a protective barrier that would be fatal to anyone who approached with hostile intentions.

And so, singly, in groups or in armies, fully aware of the risks they were taking, brave men would make their way up the desolate corpse-strewn valley towards the grim fortress on Mount Sacred—so called, because the head was kept there; and without fail they were destroyed.

The mad priest Puarata, the guardian and servant of the head, would look down from a watchtower behind the immensely strong palisades of the fortress, and would gloat over their destruction.

Only one man had come within range, and lived to tell the

tale. He survived simply because of a disability that rendered him invulnerable to the deadly power of the head: he was stone-deaf.

"It was horrible," he recounted afterwards. "We were going up the valley, moving swiftly from rock to rock, and making steady progress towards the fortress, when suddenly the ground began shaking beneath our feet and rocks began falling from the cliffs above us. I looked round at my companions and saw them writhing on the ground, with their hands clapped to their ears. In a few minutes they were dead. I can offer no explanation except that the head had killed them with magic."

But adventurers, such as he, set out for Mount Sacred, aware that the penalty for failure was death. When they did not return, many people felt that they had only themselves to blame. But the deaths of innocent people, mostly travellers, who were unlucky enough to be in the vicinity of Mount Sacred when the head was in full cry, were another matter.

People stood round in silent groups, and the same thought was in every mind. What will happen if the power of the magical head remains unchecked? Will it keep increasing until it destroys every person in the land?

Rumours began to spread from village to village, acquiring fresh and more horrific details as they went along. Before long the whole of the North Island had heard of the magical wooden head that had the power to destroy whole armies.

"Is it possible?" said Hakawau thoughtfully, when the rumours reached him. He was a very powerful priest and magician who lived in a village north of Whangaroa.

"If the rumours are true," he went on, thinking aloud, "then there can only be one man behind it all. Puarata alone has the magic to carve a head out of wood and invest it with enormous destructive powers."

Hakawau resolved to test his powers against those of Puarata. He retired to a secret cave in the heart of the bush, and there he chanted incantations that put him in a deep sleep. When he at last awoke he knew that he would conquer Puarata, because his guardian spirit had appeared to him in a dream. It was so large that its head touched the sky, while its feet rested on the ground.

"Come," he said to his trusted servant. "If we want to destroy the magical wooden head before it gets out of hand, we have no time to lose."

Hakawau and his servant at once set off, taking nothing but the mats they were wearing. They passed through Whangaroa, then went on down the coast. For many days they travelled without stopping, sometimes following the coast, sometimes crossing overland, until they reached Maraetai, where the people tried to persuade them to spend the night. When they refused, they asked them to stay for a meal.

"Oh, we ate only a little while ago," they said. "Not far from here we took some food." They were on a sacred expedition and eating would have brought them bad luck.

They continued their journey, and soon crossed the Mokau River and approached Waitara, where the servant of Hakawau became alarmed and started to wail.

"Oh, Hakawau," he cried, "let us go back. I feel the presence of evil spirits. We shall die in this place."

"We shall go on," said Hakawau, but he also felt the oppressive presence of evil spirits, hovering over them like a black cloud, and he began chanting his incantations to ward them off.

At Te Weta, Hakawau's servant again became alarmed and started wailing.

"Oh, Hakawau," he cried, "if we do not turn back now, we shall certainly die in this place."

But Hakawau chanted even more powerful incantations than before, and once more dispersed the evil spirits, so that they could go on.

They now passed through Waimatuku, where they came upon the first dead bodies. They were mostly travellers who had been walking in single file along the bush trails, when they had been struck down.

They were soon climbing a low scrub-covered hill, and were appalled at the increasing number of dead bodies they passed. All the time Hakawau kept up his incantations.

At last they reached the top of the hill, which gave them a view of Mount Sacred and the grim fortress on its summit, and there, for the first time since they left their village, Hakawau and his servant rested.

Hakawau lost no time in setting his plan in motion. Uttering his most powerful incantations, he summoned up his good spirits. Thousands upon thousands answered his call. They congregated in such dense multitudes above his head, that they cast a shimmering shadow across the sun.

Hakawau then directed the first wave of good spirits to attack the fortress, and at once they swooped in a glittering arc towards their target. There they were met by the entire force of evil spirits who had been alerted by Puarata. They headed off the good spirits and pursued them down the valley.

This was the opportunity Hakawau was waiting for. He now dispatched his second wave who made a direct attack on the unprotected fortress. The evil spirits at once swung round to come to its defence, and were caught between Hakawau's forces and utterly destroyed.

It was now quite safe to approach the fortress. Puarata saw them coming and hurried into the presence of the magical wooden head, crying aloud in supplication. "Two strangers are coming! Two strangers are coming? Destroy them! Destroy them!"

But the head had derived most of its power from the evil spirits, and now that they were dead, all it could do was to utter a low moan, and then it became silent, and never spoke again.

Puarata knew at once that he was doomed, and rushed wailing from the fortress. But the good spirits, who were waiting for just such a move, pounced on him and destroyed him. He continued his flight down the mountain as a lump of charcoal.

Meanwhile, Hakawau and his servant had reached the fortress, watched by a sullen crowd.

"You go in by the gate," said Hakawau. "I intend to show the people here my power by scaling the palisades."

And so, to the horror of the residents, Hakawau easily scaled the high palisades and dropped down into the fortress.

The people shouted angrily at him: "Why do you shame us by scaling the palisades? You should have entered the fortress in the proper manner, by coming through the gate."

But Hakawau brushed past them without a word. He sought out their sacred places and desecrated them by entering them in an impure state. The great carved head, that had once been so powerful, he knocked over with a careless thrust of his foot.

Hakawau and his servant spent many days resting in the fortress. The people cooked for them and attended to all their needs.

But one morning Hakawau decided it was time for them to return to their village in the far north.

"Let us go," he said to his servant.

The people were surprised that they were leaving, and begged them to stay longer. When Hakawau shook his head impatiently, they cried: "If you cannot stay, then eat before you go."

But Hakawau shook his head again and said, "Oh, we ate only a little while ago. Not far from here we ate some food."

He then struck with his hand the threshhold of the house where he and his servant had been living, and every one in the fortress fell dead.

Thus, Hakawau avenged on Puarata and his people the terrible slaughter caused by the magical wooden head.

The Story of Hinemoa

It was the late afternoon of what had been a very hot day. Two old women were sitting on the shore of Rotorua, enjoying the cool breezes that were now beginning to ruffle the still waters of the lake. They were weaving baskets of flax, and talking idly.

"Why, when I was a girl," said one, "we never had time to be love-sick. The men were larger than life in those days, and a girl had only herself to blame if she felt lonely. Now, look at Hinemoa — "

"Hinemoa," said the other severely, "is the highborn daughter of a great chief. She can't go scampering off into the bushes with a man, like any common slut."

"Common slut, indeed," said the first in a haughty tone. "I'll have you know my father — "

"Your father was a nobody," said the second. "Now, hush— here she comes."

Unaware that she was being discussed, Hinemoa walked along the beach, tears streaming from her eyes. She had just told her father, Amukaria, of her love for Tutanekai, and had been frightened by the change that had come over his face.

"This young man," he asked, suddenly menacing. "Have you been seeing him?"

"No, Father," she said, avoiding his eyes. "He does not even know I love him."

"Ha!" he said, contemptuously. "How can you love a man you do not even know?"

"But I do know him, Father," said Hinemoa.

"Be careful what you say," he warned.

"It was at the tribal gathering that I saw him," she said

softly. "He had come with a party from Mokoia. He is a chief, Father, and I have heard that on his island there is none to match him as a warrior."

"I do not know him," said her father, stiffly. "He does not exist."

"His eyes never once left my face," she went on dreamily, as if she had not heard him, "but how could I let him know that all the time I was aware of him? I liked his handsome looks well enough—what girl would not? But when he took his flute and played it—Oh, Father! It was then I knew I loved him."

"Enough, child," he said, impatiently. "You talk like a fool. Now hear me carefully. Forget this man, for I have plans for you more fitting to your rank. If you try to see him, I shall confine you to the house. As for Tutanekai, if he sets foot anywhere near the village he will die. Now go, and mark my words."

Now, a little later, Hinemoa was walking past the two old women, her father's words still sounding in her ears.

"Oh, Tutanekai," she cried, "what will become of us? Our love had scarcely begun—and now it seems to be over, killed by my father's cruelty. Tutanekai—if only you could talk to me! You would tell me what to do."

Then it seemed that the wind died down, and faintly above the lapping of the water she heard the sound of a flute. Soft and clear, it came across the darkening lake from the island of Mokoia.

Hinemoa stood enraptured. It was Tutanekai telling her to be brave, for he loved her and would always love her. She sat listening to him, while the moon rose above the lake and laid a white path to the island for her dreams to tread.

When she at last went home to face an angry father, still the flute kept saying, "Be brave, Hinemoa, for I shall always be near you."

Night after night she went down to the shore, and, when she heard the flute, all her loneliness and frustration would fall away, and she would become as a young girl at the feet of her lover, listening to his voice encouraging her, filling her with hope.

Her father disapproved of the way she spent her evenings. He had even tried to force her into staying indoors, but she had sat motionless for hours and wept, so that he had to give in to her.

Now, whenever he heard the flute, he would clench his fists and scowl. "If only the wind would blow from another direction. It would end all this nonsense."

He ordered his priests to use all their magical powers to turn the wind around, and when they had failed he dismissed them angrily.

Despite Amukaria's watchfulness, Tutanekai managed to get a message to her through Tiki, his closest friend. He told her what she already knew in her heart, and her joy was complete.

Her father noticed the change and became more watchful than ever. He took the added precaution of having every canoe removed from the beach and placed under guard.

Hinemoa watched unmoved, for she had already thought of a plan to outwit her father and join her lover on Mokoia. She would tie six empty gourds together as floats, and she would swim to the island.

The distance was great, and even by day it would have daunted most men. But she intended to swim by night when there would be less risk that she would be discovered.

She waited for the next moonless night, and when it grew dark she crept down to the beach. Taking off her cloak of kiwi feathers, she slipped into the water, pushed herself forward on the floats, and began swimming.

So far so good! All was quiet in the village. No one had noticed her leave.

But how cold and dark the water was! Something slimy brushed against her leg, and she almost panicked. But the voice of Tutanekai, talking through the flute, encouraged her, and she forgot her fears. On through the night she swam, until she grew so weak that several times she almost drifted off the floats, and sank. But always the flute talked to her and kept her going.

At last she felt the sharp stones of Mokoia under her feet. She dragged herself on to the beach where she lay awhile, exhausted and half-frozen. When she had recovered, she walked round the island until she found a cave warmed by a hot spring, and there she slept.

Footsteps woke her early in the morning. She looked out and

saw a slave filling a calabash with water. Had she not seen him at the tribal meeting, attending on Tutanekai?

Her eyes alive with mischief, she said, "Slave, for whom are you fetching water?"

He was startled, and almost dropped the calabash. "For Tutanekai," he said. "Are you a spirit?"

"I am thirsty," she said. "Give me a drink."

He gave her the calabash, and she drank from it, and then dashed it against a rock and broke it.

"Why did you do that?" he cried. "Now my master will beat me."

But Hinemoa said nothing, and the slave returned to the village, full of foreboding.

Tutanekai saw him arrive empty-handed, and he shouted, "Where is the water that I asked you to fetch?"

The slave opened his mouth to speak, but Tutanekai pushed a calabash into his hand and said sharply, "Fill it—and be quick about it."

Hinemoa heard him return, and waited until he had filled the calabash for the second time. Then again she asked for water, and after she had drunk from the calabash she smashed it as she did the first .

Great was Tutanekai's anger, when he heard the slave's report. Seizing his whale-bone club, he went to the cave and shouted, "Come out of there—and be prepared to die."

Then Hinemoa appeared and, with downcast eyes, she reproached him, "O Tutanekai—would you kill your wife?"

The club dropped from his hand, and joyful was his cry: "Hinemoa!"

"Hinemoa!" echoed the rocks. "Hinemoa!"

Te Houtaewa
and the Kumaras

North of Kaitaia is the tail of *Te Ika a Maui*—the narrowest part of New Zealand. In some places you can see from the road the sandhills on both sides of the island. On the west coast the Ninety Mile Beach, washed by the Tasman Sea, stretches in a smooth unbroken curve from Scott Point in the north to Ahipara in the south—a distance of some 75 miles, not 90, as you might think.

The two main tribes of the Far North are the Aupouri and Rarawa. The Aupouri live near the tip of New Zealand, in the bare, wind-beaten country round Te Kao; the Rarawa round Ahipara where the soil is better and life is easier. The story of Te Houtaewa is part of the history of both these tribes. Today they live in peace, but when our story takes place—about 1820— they were bitter enemies. Te Houtaewa is specially interesting as an example of a recent historical figure in the process of becoming a legend.

He is not one of the greatest of the Maori heroes, but the stories of his exploits make him easily the fastest runner who ever lived. An Aupouri elder told me (possibly with tongue in cheek) that he was eight feet tall and that his estimated top speed was sixty miles per hour. He also said that the great runner was able to run two lengths of the Ninety Mile Beach between high tide and low tide. Compared with him the fastest of our modern athletes would have seemed as slow as men on crutches.

So great was his fame that it spread throughout New Zealand, bringing *mana* (glory) to his tribe and arousing envy in the hearts of his enemies. When the Waikato people heard how fast he was they sent their two greatest runners to challenge him in a foot race. This took place on the Ninety Mile Beach, beginning at Hukatere. Te Houtaewa gave his challengers a start, but at Ngapai he overtook the slower of the two and, without losing any speed, he dashed out his brains with his club. Several tremendous strides brought him up to the second man whom he killed in the same way. After this, no one was so foolhardy as to challenge him again.

Te Houtaewa was an old-time Maori who honoured the traditions and customs of his ancestors. He despised the new things that the settlers were bringing into New Zealand. It is said that when his uncle returned from a visit to England he brought back a double-barrelled musket and an axe. He intended to give the musket to his nephew and keep the axe for himself. But Te Houtaewa was so horrified when he saw his uncle shoot a bird that he refused to accept the gift, saying that it was fit only for a coward. He chose the axe, which he considered a more manly weapon.

In the Far North Te Houtaewa is a legendary figure—the hero of many Maori children who have heard of his exploits from their elders. Here is the most popular story that is told about him.

Te Houtaewa used to camp with his mother at Kahokawa at the northern end of the Ninety Mile Beach. One day when she went to prepare a meal she found they had nothing to eat but dried fish and shellfish. She went to her son and told him the bad news.

"Do not worry, Mother," said Te Houtaewa, "We shall have *kumaras* with our fish. Yesterday a war party returned from the south with the news that on the hillsides at Ahipara are *kumara* pits that are left unguarded. Our enemies have so much they can surely spare us some."

His mother pleaded with him not to be so rash as to go alone into enemy territory, but he laughed at her fears and said, "Light up the fire, Mother, and before the stones are hot enough I shall be back with the *kumaras.*"

He told her to fetch him the two largest flax bags she could find and, with one in each hand, he set off. He took no weapon because he meant to rely entirely on his speed to get him out of trouble; and he ran naked so that the wind would not catch at his clothes and hold him back.

The beach stretched ahead of him, gleaming in the morning sun. He ran where the sand was firm, just beyond the reach of the breakers, his legs a blur as they devoured the miles.

Te Houtaewa's heart was full of joy. He liked nothing better than running on the beach with the sea beside him. He loved the slight give of the sand beneath his toes and the breeze whistling through his hair. Even the thought of the danger ahead of him did not reduce his pleasure. Instead it seemed to put steel springs into his legs so that each stride he took measured more than fifty feet. For mile after mile he ran tirelessly, slackening speed only when his feet became so hot with friction that he had to run into the sea to cool them off.

Within an hour he reached Ahipara and hid in the sand-hills so that he could spy out the land. It was noon and the sun was very hot. The whole village seemed to be sleeping, apart from a few dogs that were too busy tearing at a carcase to be interested in him.

In a dozen giant strides Te Houtaewa reached the *kumara* pits on the hillside, tore away the covering, and began filling the first of his bags. He had half-filled it when a Rarawa woman came out of a house and happened to look up. She recognised him at once and screamed out the alarm: "Te Houtaewa—the thief! Surround and kill him!"

Immediately the whole village was in an uproar. The children wailed, the dogs barked, and the men shouted and cursed as they ran for their weapons. They planned to surround Te Houtaewa as quickly as possible, then rush him in a body and kill him.

What a prize had fallen into their hands! The man who struck him down would be famous as the slayer of Te Houtaewa! Each man gripped his weapon more firmly as the long line moved quickly and cautiously up the hillside.

What was Te Houtaewa doing meanwhile? When the old woman cried out he had almost panicked and fled, but he reminded himself that he was Te Houtaewa who feared no man, least of all the Rarawa. Keeping an eye on the advancing men and ignoring their fierce taunts and insults, he filled his first bag and began on the second. They were now less than fifty yards away and were hurrying to encircle him. It would be very dangerous to delay any longer.

Te Houtaewa picked up the full bags, one in each hand, and looked for a gap in the cordon. He pretended to start his run, and when the Rarawa scattered he jeered at them.

He then gathered his strength and with a shout, he hurled himself down the hill with the speed of an avalanche. No man could have stood in his way and lived. The cordon gave way, and in a flash Te Houtaewa was through it and speeding towards the beach.

Halfway up the beach, he saw a flock of godwits, and he decided to catch some to take home to his mother. He put his bags down, crept as close as he could, and waited for the waves to break, for he knew that godwits always faced the breakers and were then off their guard. When that happened he swooped on them and gathered up an armful before they were aware of their danger. Satisfied with his morning's work, he hurried home to his mother, who was relieved that he had come to no harm and had brought back the *kumaras* with him.

It is said that the two bags of *kumaras* weighed forty pounds apiece, but such was Te Houtaewa's strength that his journey home took only a little longer than his journey to Ahipara.